T0300721

Ad Cogitavit

A Collection of Rational Thought

Isy Peréz

AuthorHouse™
1663 Liberty Drive
Bloomington, IN 47403
www.authorhouse.com
Phone: 1-800-839-8640

First published by AuthorHouse 2/17/2011

ISBN: 978-1-4567-4230-0 (sc)
ISBN: 978-1-4567-4229-4 (e)

Library of Congress Control Number: 2011902732

Printed in the United States of America

Dedicated to:
My Mom and Dad
Krystal-Rose Perez
Mr. and Mrs. Zamora
Mr. Cayce
THV 301
and
The Running Club

φφκα

Intro

I attended UTNIF, The University of Texas National Institute of Forensics. From here I had something of an epiphany into new ways of thinking. It was all the result of the training I received for Lincoln-Douglas debate. Being a former LD debater I am somewhat competitive and prideful of LD so feel that I must express that LD has helped me achieve writing this book infinitely more than extemp or any other event would've.

Now that that's cleared, many of these ideas have been existing in my own head and so I finally decided to put them down onto the printed word. I find ironic that I am writing a book since I have never been to big on reading books myself. I just decided to do this on a whim since my roommates in THV 301 were teasing me about writing a manifesto. This came two years after an influential high school teacher, Mr. Cayce, joked about how I should write one with the new word processing software I received.

I do not intend to change the world with this. I don't

even intend to change your own views. I simply wish to collect my royalties so that I can pay for college.

Oh and in case you were wondering when I went to UTNIF, it was the summer going into my junior year of high school. And so it begins...

PART ONE - Philosophical Thought

Chapter One - The Open Mind

I find it ironic that the people who usually tell you to have an open mind are the ones who themselves do not possess one. Nevertheless, I ask you now to open your mind. Open your mind to new ideas. Open it to logic, to reason. I feel that is the most important idea to start off with as it will be the groundwork for the following essays in this collective work.

Now, it must be noted that the current notion stating a source that is not credible ought not be taken into account is a false one. For example, if it were to be said that Adolf Hitler believed pork should be cooked properly then the idea of cooking pork properly ought not be considered evil just because Adolf Hitler is generally accepted as an evil person. Similarly if Hitler had a mustache, wearing a mustache is not an evil act. This is because neither the mustache nor the cooking of the pork is what made Hitler evil rather it was other acts he committed. This may seem ridiculous but it must first be understood in order to fully grasp the rest of the ideas that will be set forth here.

In these essays I may laud radical jihadist terrorists for dying for an idea they strongly believe in, but that does not mean I laud their ideas nor the fact that they kill innocent people in the process. I will still continue to condemn their acts and stand against them with my ideals.

Now, the reason why I must differentiate credibility of the source from the viability of an idea is because there may be many ideas in these essays that you may not agree with but that does not mean that they should holistically be discarded. Do not look at the radicalness of these ideas; rather look at the reasonableness of them. It is best to open the mind and weigh the ideas fairly. For if you close the mind, you do not better yourself as a person. You merely keep yourself shut in with stubbornness refusing to find a better way. Many people may read this and begin to think of arguments as to why it cannot be true and will reject it on face value without looking at it critically. I ask you to be unlike them, I ask you to be rational.

It is easy to call someone crazy, ridicule them and throw out their credibility. But even if credibility is lost, the ideas of the person ought not be. Look at the idea. Ask what the rational for it is. See if it works. It will take effort, but it is worth it in the end since you will have an idea that society would have lost in it being thrown away.

That addresses one problem to opening the mind, incredulity towards the source of new ideas. However, there is still the obstacle of believing old ideas simply because they come from a credible source. For matters of simple fact this may be acceptable, such as what the time is or what a score to a sports game is, but for matters of deeper knowledge and even for some other simple facts it is unacceptable. Just as Adolf Hitler was not evil in all actions a genius such as Albert Einstein may not be correct in all actions.

Experts are still human and therefore can still error. When an expert's erred opinions are taken for truth based solely on the expert's credentials, society is left with merely wronged information that could have been replaced by truth. Only if an expert's ideas are backed with reasoning should they be taken as truth. For instance, if a person writes 5 books on ethics, this does not necessarily mean that his opinion ought to be weighed higher than a person who has never written a book without even looking at both sides' reasoning. It is the reasoning behind the argument and not the credibility from which it comes. The writer could just as possibly be wrong as the regular person; it takes an analysis of the ideas in order to make an accurate judgment.

If anything hopefully this essay encourages you to analyze ideas and viewpoints from a much more critical standpoint.

Chapter Two - The Necessity of the Existence of God

Many have argued for the existence of God. Many have argued against such existence. Both of these arguments have been in vain as the existence or the inexistence of a deity cannot be proven solidly since the idea of God is one which goes beyond our understanding as human beings. We cannot draw conclusions on what we cannot see. We can only draw inferences and inferences are not solid enough to draw proof for the existence or inexistence of God. Therefore all arguments pertaining to whether there is an omnipotent being are inherently a wash.

Furthermore, those who believe in God ought not need proof of his existence. Faith alone should suffice for their belief. The beauty of religion is that it cannot be proven yet people still devote their lives to it based solely on faith. It is the faithful whom we ought to mimic.

Therefore, I will not argue that God exists. Rather, I

will argue that we ought to believe in the existence of a God based upon the rationality of the necessity of such belief.

It is first valuable to note that it is more prudent to believe in the existence of a God and to be religious rather than unreligious. This is because if there is a God and you believe in him then you are more likely to be better off in the afterlife. However, if there is not a God and you believe so then you will not necessarily be better off in an afterlife. Therefore it is better to believe based solely on the fact that religion offers possible advantages whereas lack of religion provides none.

We as humans need a rational code. That is to say we need a set standard to determine what is right and what is wrong. For example, if one person is to argue to another that he ought not kill another person what ground does the first person have to say that murder is necessarily wrong? Well, he could argue that murder is wrong since it decreases the population, but then why is decreasing the population wrong. It could then be argued that decreasing the population is wrong since it reduces our society's productivity, but then why is that wrong. As you can see this line of questions leads to an Aesop gap where nothing can be proven finitely in actuality. Therefore we can never label anything as wrong because there would be no set reason why it would be wrong.

Another avenue the first person could have taken in arguing for the wrongness of murder is to say it is an inherent right for all humans to be guaranteed their lives. However, how can this be valid if the Aesop gap, as explained before, exists? It cannot be inherently given to us that we must accept the right of all humans to have their lives without that right being proven. Why is that a right? The only explanation, the only way to bridge the gap, the only way the first person can prove that murder is in fact wrong, as we as a society know it to be, is the existence of God and the code given to us by God. Now, I do not suggest that the code is necessarily the Bible, Qur'an, Tanakh, Upanishads or even the religious doctrines many religions hold today. Rather, the code God gives each of us is within us. It is our rationale to determine that murder is inherently wrong without needing proof, it is how we know stealing is wrong without needing proof, it is our conscience which tells us what is right and what is wrong. God tells us it is wrong and tells us what we ought to want.

Without this compass God provides we can easily fall into nihilistic skepticism where the gap prevails, nothing can be proven and no ground can be made in any argument. Because the gap theory shows us how nothing can be proven in this world, we need a stable entity, God, to provide us with traction so that we can tread forward on this otherwise icy path. God and the code he provides are the set standards that we can use to measure ideas and thoughts, it provides us with stability. We as faithful people must also always have a sort of truth to make our faith worthwhile. Otherwise, these essays and all essays of argument are pointless since they may or may not be right and are just as likely either way.

Chapter Three - Objectivism vs. Altruism

It is important in any intellectual conversation to acknowledge Ayn Rand's theory of Objectivism. She contrasts this to Altruism, a selfless belief that an individual's actions ought to be aimed at helping out society and that the value of society ought to outweigh the individual's own benefit. Ayn Rand and her Objectivist school of thought would argue against such selflessness saying how one ought to look for their own objectives.

While objectivists may be incredibly logical and smart, their downfall is their arrogance as they overlook an amazing flaw in objectivism. Objectivists argue that the individual ought to seek their own welfare above the society's. However, the Objectivist justifies this position by arguing how seeking one's own objectives betters society by progressing it. At this moment, Ayn Rand and the entire Objectivist community concede that society is the best value one can achieve as they themselves try to achieve it in order to justify their beliefs.

By trying to improve society by progressing it, Objectivists are merely Altruists themselves as they are striving for what is best for the society. The reason for this is because what is best for society is inherently best for the individual.

Objectivism is equivalent to Altruism in its aims. Objectivism however believes that holding one individual over the other better achieves this aim. This cannot be so since it has been proven time and again that working as an individual is infinitely less productive than working as a team. Objectivism's main object is to attain progress therefore it would only fail in its main object and should not be looked to.

We know that working as a single individual who is wholly credited for his own actions is not productive by looking at several examples. It is interesting that in the Cold War, the way we defeated the collectivist oriented Soviets was through teamwork. We saw this in sports with our teamwork in the 1980 Olympic hockey team that defeated the Soviets, with our teamwork in NASA that achieved reaching the moon faster, and with our superior armed forces that were built on teamwork. Objectivism neglects these empirical warrants that show how working as a collective unit better achieves society's goals than working as an individual.

The objectivist will try to argue that individuals are coerced into carrying an entire society with their work. However, this is another falsity as it presupposes that each work of an individual is independent of another's. Ayn Rand loves to use the example of Prometheus's invention of fire. Prometheus was punished for it and society reaped the benefits off of Prometheus's labor. However, Prometheus required the reaping of benefits off of the person who discovered the fuel to the fire. John Galt reaped the benefits off of the work of the person who first invented a motor. Each work, each invention is built off of another, we do not have the invention of the airplane without the invention of the engine we do not have the invention of the engine without the controlled explosion and we do not have explosions without Prometheus's fire.

Now, this isn't to say that persons who invent things ought not be rewarded. Society ought to help those who help society, it is only fair. This is an idea that objectivists also assert and it may be the only one which is true. The individual ought to be rewarded for his work, but it should still be noted that the individual would not have achieved his work without the help of the society. It should also be noted that the society would not have been able to help out the individual without a previous contribution from another individual. Therefore, we can see that the individual and society create a symbiotic relationship. This means that radical schools of thought that stress the importance of collectivism or individualism are only have half of the truth. The whole picture contains both collectivism and individualism working together. All debates between the two ideas are moot as they are both partially correct.

As far as creativity, the society is best served by allowing the individual to express creative ideas, as each may be a new way to improve the society as a whole. This seems to be a truth, which is common sense enough to be self-evident. The society ought to promote creative thinking that improves the society as a whole.

Chapter Four - Love and Sex

The subject of love is one that is so complex in its simplicity. It is one that is so ambiguous. Some feel the only way to gain knowledge of the subject is through experience however there are some truths to it that can be seen regardless of any sort of experience.

Love, the attainment of it from another as well as its reciprocated offering to another, is the greatest of all accomplishments any human being can strive for. It ought to be the main goal for all humans and for mostly all of us it is. A majority of our actions can be seen as means to our end goal of attaining love. Some may try to be super rich, super good-looking, super social and they do it all to expand their choices and thus their odds of finding someone who they can love and who will love them in return.

It is clear that love is the attainment of happiness when looking at it truthfully as all experiences with love are much better than without love. Our society today would tell us that settling down with one person is something of a taboo and that the ultimate goal we can attain is to have sex with the most number of partners and the most good-looking of partners. However, to have sex promiscuously is to devalue what the gift of sex is while lowering the possibility of actually finding someone to love who will give love in return.

Many question what love is. As stated before it is something which is so simple but powerful. It is so powerful that we cannot comprehend just how simple it is. It is quite simply our want to be in union with another person. There is a religious reason for this which will be discussed later.

The best form to solidify love is through sex as it connects the body joining it with the mind and heart which are both already in union between the two people. There is such a euphoria during sex that many try to have it without first having love. However this is like watching the end of a movie without watching the entire movie. Sure the ending of The Sixth Sense may have been great, but it would've been significantly less of a thriller had only the climax been shown. Therefore, it makes sense to first be in love before having sex.

Chapter Five - Challenging the Status Quo

Perhaps it is our society today, perhaps it is human nature, but a quality that seems prevalent amongst many of us is to accept the status quo. This is to say that many ideas that have been in place for long enough are not questioned for their worth. Examples of this in ideology include, labeling Communism as inherently wrong or labeling Democracy as inherently good.

The problem that arrises from this is that in not questioning our beliefs we forget why certain things are good or bad and so when new ideas surface that are similar in bad qualities but not in face value, the society falls for the very thing they "knew" to be inherently bad. Similarly an idea with good qualities but that has the face appearance of what seems bad may not be applied helping the society to improve.

An example of this in present day discourse is in the healthcare debate. Many claim that this is "socialism", but do not realize what it is that makes socialism wrong. Instead they see socialism as an inherent evil when many industrialized nations such as France are perfectly fine be socialistic societies. This is not to say that socialism is necessarily good only that tagging it on an idea is not enough to claim the idea as evil. Instead what one ought to do is ask why is socialism evil? Why is freedom good? Why are taxes bad? If people do not ask these questions, if they do not find out why certain things which they have always known to be good or bad are in fact that way, then arbitrary labels of good and bad will be misplaced on ideas looking to improve or destroy our society.

The other arena where the status quo ought to be challenged is in the pragmatic, every day world. Many consider it a difficulty to write a book when anyone can really do it. Many consider the stock market too complicated to get involved. People take many things for granted and instead of fixing the problems they face, they only shy away from finding the solution.

People instead ought to ask why things are the way they are. Why is it so difficult to publish a book? Why must the stock market be the way it is? How do I fix it? People must become problem solvers otherwise they fall to stagnation and the problems that face them today will continue to face them forever.

With my final statements in this first part, I call you to change something. Find a problem which faces you today. Find something that makes you unhappy. Solve it.

PART TWO -
Theological Thought

Chapter One - The Simplification of God

Over the years, many theologians have written immense arguments in their field arguing one way or another for what the will of God is, what his nature is and what we are to do for him. The curiousness of this is that it is all very simple, so simple that the commonest of men could figure it out.

In the First Letter to the Corinthians we are told God has given us three gifts; faith, hope and love. In the four Gospels we are told Jesus would like us to uphold one thing above all, love. There is a theme throughout the spiritual writings of the Bible that come through time and again; The positive attitudes of Faith, Love, Perseverance and Humility always triumph over the negative attitudes of stubbornness, arrogance and hate.

Quite simply, it is one thing we are to do which fulfills our religious obligation, love. Love embodies the other positive attitudes and is only done when the other attitudes accompany it. If you are to love someone, you are to have faith in them, near blind faith if not blind. If you are to love someone you will persevere for them because of your faith in them. If you love someone you will not belittle them with your patronizing arrogance.

We are to love ourselves, each other and our God. This is the simple standard by which we ought to measure Christian Theological debate. We are to have love for one another and to encourage love amongst each other, to care for every human being to the best of our ability. This is the simplicity of God.

Chapter Two - Sex and Marriage

The Catholic church and many other Protestant churches have declared that it is a sin to have pre-marital sex. Let's look at why this is so. As argued earlier, sex ought not be had unless the two people having it are in love. There are many reasons why not to have promiscuous loveless sex that are used as stock arguments such as STDs or the risk of a pregnancy that is not welcome. Today these arguments are easily countered with modern contraception that makes the spread of STDs and the risk of pregnancy negligible in the eyes of the persons using the contraception.

However, there is another argument which is the most powerful against having loveless sex and pertains only to loveless sex. The argument is that the sex is simply empty and altogether unsatisfying. This is the argument touched upon in the Philosophical Thought chapter covering love and sex.

The reason why sex is empty and meaningless when it is had without love has much to do with God. Our ultimate goal is to be in union with God; That is our salvation. Love is the emotional bond two people can make, it is completed with sex which creates the physical bond. Because every human being is created in God's image and is a temple of the lord, it can be said that each of us has a very small piece of God and his love within us. Therefore, when one person is emotionally bonded to another and completes that bond with sex, the completion itself is a very small glimpse of heaven as it is similar to being in union with God but on a much smaller scale. However, this glimpse cannot and does not occur unless there is already an emotional bond as the glimpse only happens upon the momentary completion of being in union. Likewise, the emotional bond itself cannot give the glimpse as it is not enough to bring two people into union with one another.

With this knowledge it is easy for us to see that it is more logical for the different churches to condemn loveless marriage and not pre-marital marriage as not all marriages necessarily have two people who actually love each other and not all those who are in love are married. The different churches ought to support the fulfilling sex and condemn that of emptiness and worthlessness as the former provides for a closer glimpse of having achieved salvation.

Perhaps the different churches meant for this to be the actual case as it ought to be assumed that those who are married are assuredly in love and those who are not married may not be. However, it must be recognized that marriage is not synonymous with love since there are many empirical examples of one existing independently without the other. It is much more reasonable to replace the word marriage with love in many doctrines concerning sex.

For example, the different churches' condemnation of adultery should not be a condemnation of having sex with a married person or being married and having sex with someone you are not married to. Rather, it ought to extend to condemning with someone who is in love with another or having sex with someone you are not in love with. This is because a man cheating on his wife who has no emotional bond with him at all has much less emotional impact as a man cheating on a woman he loves who loves him back even if the second couple is not married.

However, this argument is not to condone loveless marriages either. Rather, it is to redefine marriage as an act or sacrament where society and the community can acknowledge and celebrate the already existing love. It is a human recognition of what God has already done.

Now, this love can exist in all forms. This is to say that homosexuality may be permitted under the eyes of God if the two men or women love each other. This is a huge topic of debate since many people share different beliefs on the matter. I will leave this open for debate as those who are for gay marriage will have the burden of proving there is the existence of love in the relationship and those who are against it must prove that there is only the illusion of love or that no love exists at all. I will not take a side on the matter as I do not know enough and would only be spewing ignorant arguments. I will only frame the topic for further discussion.

Chapter Three - Contraception

Birth control methods such as a condoms have become widely accepted among many Protestant denominations in the Christian faith. The Catholic Church, however, still rejects the notion that any artificial form of contraception is permissible under God's law. Since this is a pressing debate in the religious community it is important to look at it more closely.

Many Catholic believers assert that artificial contraception is wrong for many reasons. Before looking at these reasons we must first divide birth control into two groups, pre-conception birth control and post-conception birth control. Post-conception birth control, because of its very nature, can be and ought to be considered equivalent to abortion as it destroys a fetus that would otherwise eventually grow to a postnatal person. There is an apparent consensus here then as almost no Christian denomination condones abortion.

Therefore, our focus in the matter ought to be on pre-conception birth control. The objections that are made by those who believe birth control to be sinful are as follows:

1. Sex is for the purpose of procreation, therefore taking out procreation devalues sex rendering it useless.
2. It lowers the risks that come with promiscuity inadvertently encouraging such loveless sex.
3. It is in direct opposition to God's will taking him out of the equation when deciding when life begins.

It is with these three contentions that the affirmation is made that it is a sin to use contraception.

Looking at the first contention, we can see that this cannot be as it has already been established that the sole purpose for sex is not procreation as the undismissible reason is the solidification of love and union with another person to gain a glimpse of what being in union with God is like. It is only in this great amount of love that another human being is created. Therefore, this is not a valid reason as sex has purpose beyond procreation.

The second contention put forth is one that ought to be taken seriously as we do not want to condone the continued spread of the culture of promiscuity and loveless sex. The harms promiscuity brings devalue what the purpose of sex is. Therefore, it seems reasonable to make using contraception impermissible since the absence of it presents the risk of a pregnancy which the promiscuous people are not prepared for. However, it can be seen that, because contraception is sinful for what it brings as a result, this contention does not show how contraception is wrong in itself but only in how it may be used.

Therefore, this second contention has two flaws. The first is that not all people who use contraceptive devices during sexual intercourse are promiscuous meaning the contraceptive cannot possibly be sinful since it did not provide for a graver sin in consequence. The second is that it can be assumed that those who engage in promiscuity against the Church's will are more likely to go against that will again in using contraceptives. Declaring contraceptives wrong will not decrease promiscuity. This second contention also suggests that the risks contraception lowers are all that deters promiscuity. It should be acknowledged that some things are wrong in themselves and not because of their risks. Therefore, by this contention, artificial contraceptives can be fine on an individual basis so long as they are not being used to promote loveless sex.

The last contention is that we as humans begin the process of playing God when we choose when a life is born and when it is not. To this, God can still choose if a life is conceived as the result of sexual intercourse with an artificial contraceptive as the contraceptive is not always successful in its purpose. Secondly, the alternative to a contraceptive is to not have sex which is always successful in preventing a pregnancy. Therefore, it is better to have sex and use a contraceptive than to not have sex by this argument since by having sex there is still a possibility for God to choose for a life to be conceived.

Now when looking at the arguments for God's law permitting contraception, there aren't any that seem overwhelmingly convincing. The central argument that is used is that promiscuity is inevitable, therefore we might as well say that contraception is not a sin so that people can at least have safe sex. This thought process inadvertently condones promiscuity which is in itself a sin, therefore the argument there condones and even promotes sin. This argument is different than the attack just placed on the Catholic Church's second contention as it focuses on allowing people to have promiscuous sex safely whereas the argument two paragraphs ago focuses on allowing people to have love filled sex safely. It is then a sin to use a contraceptive when having promiscuous sex.

However, there is another argument which must be looked at and that is the couple who loves each other, would like to solidify their love through the act of sexual intercourse, but does not have the means to raise a child whether it be economic reasons or simple lack of will to raise a child. This is a difficult case to discern as it gives us an unusual look at the debate of quality of life vs life itself. Now, many who are pro-choice argue that sometimes the couple cannot raise a child and so ought to have the right to prevent a poor life for the child. However, it has been agreed upon in the Christian community that the child's life is much more important in God's eyes than the quality of life that child has. However, now we ask is a potential life which has not even been conceived as valuable to protect as the one which has already been conceived?

To this I say no. Before conception a life does not yet exist and so therefore there is no soul there and there is no person to take away the right to life from. Life begins at the point of conception, therefore, contraceptives which act before conception and not after, are not sinful to use. This is a default judgment since there is nothing that makes contraceptives bad in and of themselves, however this is not to say that contraceptives are justified to be used by any means. They are simply there to use for a couple.

Now, although they may not be sinful, it may be better to not use contraceptives as it will show that the couple has faith in God to provide in the event the couple has children they cannot support by economic, social or any other means. It is always best to have faith in God and to let his will be done therefore, the use of contraceptives is not evil enough to be called a sin but it may be better in God's eyes not to use them.

Chapter Four - Arrogance and Humility

One of the best lessons of the Bible is that of Humility over Arrogance. It is interesting because there is a balance asked for by God. He asks that we be humble and modest, but not so much so that we lose our faith. He asks that we be faithful in God's ability to give us strength but not so much so that we become arrogant.

God promises us that he will exalt the humble and strike down those who are arrogant. This is a very interesting take on things. It is because God wants to be the one who will make us happy. He does not want us to be content with ourselves. If material items make us happy, we have no need for God. If reason makes us happy, we have no reason for God. For what person calls the fire department when he doesn't think his house is on fire. Therefore, God would like us to be humble so that we will be closer to him and call on him more.

This is also an interesting philosophy on life to take.

If one always thinks he is not good enough, he can always improve. An athlete perfects his sport, but when he thinks his playing is perfect he becomes complacent and allows for another athlete to become better, another athlete who continued to think he wasn't good enough. The moment we become arrogant and think we have all the answers is the moment we lose our ability to get any better.

Socrates was declared the most intelligent person by an oracle in Ancient Greece. He did not believe it and wanted to find out who the most intelligent person really was. It was because of his denial that he was so intelligent. He could outwit any merchant, lawyer or politician because he accepted that he did not know everything when the rest claimed they did. The best leaders do not want their position. George Washington did not want praise. Rather, he wanted to live quietly in his Virginian home. These are just two famous examples of how being humble is better in the long run than being arrogant. It is almost common-sensical yet many people still practice arrogance before humility. We must work to be humble, this is especially true in debating ideas.

Remember that you are no better than anyone else, that God will love the "sinner" at the bar or strip club as much as you. You're place is not to put the "sinner" in his or hers. Your place is not to look down your nose at the "sinner" in a condescending manner. Your place is to love the "sinner" just as God loves you, because you are the "sinner" as I am.

Chapter Five - The Ten Commandments

It is asked of Jesus in the Gospels which of the ten is the greatest commandment. To this Jesus replies that we all ought love each other and that that is the greatest of commandments. This is seen largely as God telling us that so long as we love each other we will follow the commandments. However, it is something greater than this alone.

It is first important to note that each of the commandments act in concert with each other to reinforce central ideas that God wants us to understand. The First and Third commandments are the clearest example of this as God tells us he wants to be number one in our hearts and then asks us to keep the Sabbath so that we can forget the entire world for one day so that we might focus on our union with God. In order to keep the Sabbath we must have God as number one in our lives. If there is a football game that we'd rather watch or some workshop we'd rather attend than keep the day to God then we obviously don't value God above all things. Therefore, in order to do one, you must do the other.

This is the same as how the Ten Commandments interact with the so called "Golden Rule". In order to fulfill any of the Ten Commandments successfully, love must be the motivating factor. In order to love everyone as yourself you must uphold the Ten Commandments. Keeping any one of the ten without love as motivation, with a sinister motive, with resentment or even with apathy does not allow one to fulfill the commandments as God intended. The Sabbath cannot be kept with a sort of resentment, we must look forward to it to achieve the completeness of God's command. We cannot bare feelings of wishing to kill our brothers and sisters and resent that we cannot. Instead we must love our brothers and sisters celebrating that they are not dead.

Now looking on more in depth at the Ten Commandments, the commandments seem to imply a very strict following is demanded of us. However, God places these commandments as guidelines to make our union with him easier to accomplish. God realizes that it is difficult for us to set aside a day to dedicate to him so there is one chosen for us so that it becomes a part of our routine and almost second nature to concentrate on union with God. Therefore, a strict following of going to mass every Sunday isn't necessarily what God wants from us so much as a dedicated effort. What this means is that breaking any one of these commandments is not an evil and sin in of themselves. Rather, there end result of what this breaking of the commandment leads to can potentially be and very often is evil and leads to a decay in our relationship with God.

Essentially the standard which can be attached to the decision of what is a sin and what isn't is achieving union with God. And so long as God sees that the true motivation for one's actions are the completion of that union, he will not see it as evil.

Chapter Six - The Problem of Evil

A problem that most Atheistic thinkers will push forward in an existence of God debate is the "The Problem of Evil." The question presented is, "If there is an all-powerful and all-loving God, why does he allow evil to exist in our world?" The argument that derives from this question is that since there is evil in the world an all-powerful, all-loving God cannot exist. However, the evil which exists in our world can be explained.

Relativity is the first concept to note during this explanation. Upon entering a workout gym for the first time, one would notice that there are others there who have worked out for much longer, who are much fitter, who may even be body builders. These body builders would be able to lift heavy weights, bench pressing unworldly numbers in pounds. Then the Average Joe, having just entered the gym for the first time in his life, would attempt to lift less than his own body weight and would struggle. To him the weight would be too heavy to lift, but to the body builder, the lifting would require the same effort as lifting a paper weight.

This example is to show how different perceptions of what is difficult to handle can be created due to past experiences and other factors. Now we can see also that pain is relative. When a patient is explaining to their doctor how bad their pain is using a scale of 1-10, the patient can only use what he has experienced with pain and what he has learned of pain from others to complete this rating. Therefore, we cannot truly know what pain is and similarly what evil is because we cannot gain a truthful hold that is beyond a perception based relative opinion on what evil is and what pain is.

With this established, we can see that what we may see as evil may not even be that evil. There could be a much greater evil beyond our perception that we don't even know about. If Evilness was to be measured in a spectrum, perhaps the amount we've been exposed to is but a microscopic fraction of what evil could exist. This must be true since evil can theoretically be infinite. Therefore, how do we know that God has not cut down how much evil we experience as human beings? How do we know that God has not prevented much greater evils from happening to us? We cannot see the good that God has done for us in this area. All that we can see is the evil he has not prevented. This is like someone coming into a room and blaming a janitor for missing a spot when in reality there was a much larger mess that the person coming into the room would never know about since he had never seen the full mess the room had before.

Now if we never know the fullness of what evil is we will always complain about minimal evil the same way the person complains about the missed spot. Even this missed spot has a purpose, though. When it is cleaned, the person can then marvel at the cleanliness of the room. Similarly, the evil that is in our world is present so that it can make clean or good moments in our lives, moments which we can fully appreciate. How can a person without evil in their world, without sorrow in their lives, ever be happy? This is impossible since they will never be able to appreciate the blessings they have. Therefore, what we complain about is itself a blessing.

PART THREE - Political Thought

Chapter One - Republicans, Democrats and Whigs

The very first essay in this collection discussed the open mind when it came to everyday thought. Likewise, the open mind will be touched upon here. There is no place that a mind of openness is needed more than in the world of politics. In order for any sort of real progress to be made in our government, or in any government which relies upon multiple consents, an open mind must be utilized and people must be willing to make concessions if necessary.

Henry Clay once stated that our society is based on mutual concession; that unless one is above the weakness and infirmities of humanity he must not disdain compromise. This is from one of America's greatest politicians who always seemed to keep a sense of sanity and civility in politics during the 1800s despite militant abolitionist, anti-slavery and pro-slavery politicians who sought only to achieve their own agenda without waiver.

Today, sanity seems to be lost in politics. However, it

also seems to be in the nature of politics that sanity will not be there. The problem lays in that we as a society do not always uphold the burden of mutual concession that Henry Clay outlined for us. Rather, we myopically look at what it is that we want with little regard for how it affects others. We ought to take others' interests into account due to the theory of mutually assured destruction. If one side gains all the power to make decisions and uses this power to make decisions that benefit their party while harming the other, who's to say the oppressed party will not retaliate when it has attained power.

Such is how the Republican and Democratic parties have been acting. The most recent example being the hatred and lack of civil discourse directed at President George W. Bush. Many Republicans took the attacks personally and stood by their president regardless of the criticisms. When Obama was elected to the presidency, those type of Republicans vehemently rejected the 44th president. Any faux paw that President Obama made was pointed at with the call carrying the tone of, "See, you're guy can't do it either." That attitude is where the problem lies.

I do not blame Republicans or Democrats for this attitude, I blame those who treat their political parties as if they were a sports team. Politics should be without personified attacks as they draw out so much emotion in people that their minds become closed to logic. This is a two part critique in that blame lies on those who attack as well as those who take the attacks. The reaction that is given by those who take personal attacks is not always the best.

There are obvious personal attacks made such as placing a Hitler mustache on a person's portrait. There are also less obvious forms of personal attacks. Placing someone's name in front of an idea which you are to vilify simply to take the idea and its creator down with one attack is a personal attack. This is the case with the term "Obamacare" used in to refer to the reformations made by congress in the field of healthcare. Dissenters aim to discredit the idea by poisoning it's source, but as stated before, an idea ought not be criticized based on where it came from, rather, based on how logical it is.

Now, there are benefits to the current two-party system in America today. Anything the Republicans propose the Democrats will look at critically and anything the Democrats propose the Republicans will look at critically. Many criticize this saying it takes longer to get things done. This is true, but this isn't bad. Long calculated decisions which are looked at critically are usually the best in the long-run. Because of the animosity between the two parties, a bad policy rarely can pass through the gauntlet of criticisms they opposing party will have.

When the parties do work together, they work quicker but increase the possibility for error. This can be seen with the example of the USA PATRIOT Act which made it through congress quicker than most pieces of legislation due to the immense bipartisanship, but ended up relatively bad with 0 convictions of terrorists and questionably unprecedented constitutional violations. Had the partisanship and animosity been there, the Democrats would have not jumped on board with the Act and would have looked at it much more critically.

So it is clear now that there are tradeoffs in partisanship and bipartisanship. With Bipartisanship comes speed in legislation but a greater chance of a bad law and with Partisanship comes slower speed but better lawmaking. During times of war and distress, Bipartisanship may be necessary. However, so long as there is time to make a rational decision, we ought to thank the critical eyes that the two-parties give us so long as those critical eyes are focused on the logic and rational of an idea and not its source.

So both of the parties are necessary to see the other's flaws, but there is still a need for a third party to weigh the arguments from both sides and create the compromise called for by Henry Clay. The best examples of people who could be part of this party which would be the arbitrators of congress are Joe Lieberman and pre-'08 John McCain who sought to find compromise. This party ought not have control of congress, rather should always be a minority. This party will be the voice of reason in congress, the tiebreaker, independent of self-interests. This party ought to be the Modern Whig Party which is growing in number. The reason why it should be a completely new party is so that voters can recognize these candidates as arbiters.

The Whigs should never have a majority in Congress since they themselves ought not have a real platform, rather they ought to take the problems brought up by the Republicans and Democrats and solve them. That ought to be the extent of their aims, not power, not any other sort of ulterior motives. They are to look at the arguments from both sides, find the truth and remain faithful to it.

Chapter Two - Religion and the State

It is said that there ought to be a separation of church and state. This contention derives from the fact that the United States has written into its constitution that, "Congress shall make no law respecting an establishment of religion..." Upon looking at this clause, it would appear as though congress and thus our government ought to remain secular and without a religion. However, this in itself would be favoring a religious belief, Atheism.

Now, many would argue that Atheism is not a religion as it is in fact the absence of religion. Though Atheism may not technically be a religion, the way we perceive its functionality qualifies it as a religion and allows us to group it in with other beliefs about a higher being. It is the same when one comes across a box of Crayola markers with 8 assorted colors. Is that box lying because one of those colors is black, the absence of color? No, because we perceive black's functionality to be the same as a color even though it is the absence of color.

Atheism is the absence of religion so therefore it's establishment occurs when there is no other religion established. However, if another religion is established by congress then it has also violated the constitution. Therefore, the Establishment Clause is inherently impossible to enforce since it allows no viable action for Congress to take without being in violation of it.

Therefore, it is prudent to have a government which acknowledges the existence of God and respects his existence. The reasoning for this is outlined in the argument for the necessity of a belief in God. (*Necessity of God*)

Now, there are still those who would argue that tying any one religion to a government would end badly as it would lead to the persecution of those who did not practice the chosen religion. However, having a single religion without the allowance of others is just as harmful of an extremist view as having a completely secular government. The government should never choose one religion and mandate it. The reasoning for this is the same that Jon Stuart Mill uses in his arguments in On Liberty for free speech. Each religion is similar to an idea and must be freely expressed so that its collision with other religions allows for the logical revelation of the best religion.

Therefore, the government ought to acknowledge God, maybe even acknowledge Jesus as the messiah, but it ought not require that everyone believe such.

Still there are those who will argue that any sort of religion is malevolent in nature and so ought not exist in any sort of discourse in order to keep such discourse civil. These people will point to extremist Islamic terrorists who use suicide bombing to push their agenda. They point to extremist Christians who murder abortion doctors. They point fanatical Protestants and Catholics that are consistently violent towards one another.

It is argued that the moment religion is brought into debate, discourse is ruined because the extremist will simply say, "My God is better than your God. The Bible says you're wrong!" How can anyone have a civil conversation with such a person? Isn't it obvious that taking away religion would solve this problem?

That is where the argument falls just short of where its actual stated problem is. The argument is so myopic in scope that it forgets other similar situations where people do not argue rationally, rather they point to a "sacred" text and say all who go against it are evil. There is a group today witch hunting all who go against their sacred text, against those who wrote them. This group's name, the Tea Party worships the sacredness of the Constitution and praises the founding fathers who wrote it. Their extremist refusal to listen to reasoned arguments is nothing different of religious Bible Thumper's.

We see with this prime example of how you can have the same results as religious extremist without even having religion. Therefore the problem cannot lie within religion, rather it lies in the stubbornness of humanity and the unwillingness to look at arguments rationally, rather than embracing them without even fully understanding them.

If we were to pin this flaw in humanity on religion, we would completely be missing the flaw. We would simply be sweeping it underneath the rug while claiming we'd solved the problem. This does us no good as it impedes our progress of solving the actual problem we have at hand. It merely becomes a distraction. By saying that religion is the cause of fanaticism, we only make it that much harder to solve it.

Now that we know it is not religion which makes discourse uncivil but close-mindedness, the argument on religion in discourse then turns to a question of how its possible to argue with someone's religion. When arguing religious morals it is important to remember that the religious morals are just another set of standards by which arguments are measured. Other forms of standards are criminal law, the US Constitution or even the rules of MLB.

The standard ought to be appropriately related to the topic of discussion. If there is a dispute about whether a baseball is fair or foul, it is reasonable to use the standard of the rules of the MLB over the US Constitution as the MLB is more relevant to the discussion then the US Constitution. Therefore, if the discussion is not relevant to religion then one can simply dispute it even being used as a standard.

Even if a case can be made that religious morals are a relevant standard and they do become the measuring tool to weigh arguments, civil discourse can still be made. Some will argue that once religion is brought in, the person who introduces religion will have a full advantage. How can I argue with what his God says? Such is the argument contesting the use religious morals as a standard. The answer to this is quite simple, it is the same way we argue with the constitution or MLB rules in that we make arguments gaining ground in those areas.

Examples of arguing with someone on religiously moral grounds are as such: A Christian arguing that God hates homosexuals and that they ought to be punished here on Earth. A simple argument can be made that while Leviticus may condemn homosexuals, the Gospels add that we ought to love all of our neighbors and ought nought judge them as evil. Secondly, a Hindu argues that he knows what is best for the country and that we ought to only listen to his interpretation of Hindu writings. A simple argument can be made that the Upanishads condemn the pundits and praise the ones who do not boast their knowledge.

It may be tougher to argue on religiously moral grounds due to the probability of a lack of knowledge in all religious beliefs, but it is not impossible and it ought not be overlooked do to its toughness. We should never say it cannot be done out of laziness because then we do not progress.

Chapter Three - Censorship

John Stuart Mill wrote about censorship and free speech in On Liberty. In this piece he discussed that the ability to speak freely within a society is key to the society and finding the truth our at least what the best idea is. He argues this in saying that if an idea is true and correct, then censoring it would harm society as it would deprive us all of that correct and true idea. If the idea is bad and wrong then it is also best to keep the idea uncensored since seeing it in the light of the correct ideas will only make bright the wrongness of the bad ideas while strengthening resolve in the correct idea.

I agree with Mill's first point. However, his second point is great in a society which is capable enough to discern all ideas with a critical enough eye to see the flaws in the bad ideas. This is where we run into a problem as not everyone has the ability to do such. Whether it be lack of time, interest or concentration, not all people have the ability. We can see this with such examples as the NAZI Party in Germany. It was aloud to speak freely in to an angry population desperate for a solution and, for the most part, the population was unable to see that the party's ideas were not all good. It is with this case that some government's have decided to ban certain political parties and certain political groups. This can be good as it is sometimes necessary for the government to protect its citizens from harmful ideas.

Now, this isn't to say that we are to completely allow our government to actively burn Mein Kempf or act as though NAZIsm never existed. To do this is to forget history and the lessons it taught us. This is simply to say that we ought not allow certain harmful viewpoints to be expressed and some less harmful but potentially harmful viewpoints to be balanced by a counterpoint.

Now, we cannot arbitrarily say that a viewpoint is harmful without really knowing what harmful is. Therefore, a good example of a harmful viewpoint that ought to be censored by the government is that of religiously zealous protestors picketing soldiers' and others' funerals while chanting that the deceased deserved to die. This viewpoint is harmful as its expression causes direct harm to the deceased's loved ones who are mourning the loss. Therefore, this idea ought to be completely censored by the government. It is however, a slippery slope to say one idea causes enough distress to be censored so only distress as extreme as this case ought to constitute enough harm to censor an idea.

The second instance is the idea that has the possibility of presenting harm to others' in the society at hand. This idea need not be completely barred as the idea which causes direct harm is but ought only be allowed in circumstances that allow for its counterpoint. These potentially harmful ideas are of the nature of the previously mentioned Mein Kempf. It is a radical idea that if enacted would harm society severely. Because of the convincing nature of many of these potentially harmful ideas, a counter idea needs to be presented to show why the potentially harmful idea is not a good one. If the potentially harmful idea is left alone to be the sole option for the person discerning, the bad idea has an unfair advantage over the seemingly non-existent good idea.

If left uncontested, these ideas can go on to bring devastation to the society. The floating ideas of hateful racism can be blamed for such things as the Ku Klux Klan. The hateful anarchist ideas against the government can be blamed for terroristic acts such as the Oklahoma City Bombing. The radical anti-industrial revolution thoughts of Ted Kaczynski brought about his spree of terror. When bad ideas of hate create disciples because the lack of a counterpoint they result in real world impacts. It is one thing for John Stuart Mill and other free speech advocates to argue how censorship of ideas limits society's intellect. It is something completely different for the lack of censorship to be the cause of body bags.

Therefore, the government ought to be allowed to censor certain potentially harmful ideas where it is impossible to ensure that a counter argument will be discussed. What situations theses entail are for the elected officials to debate and decide. One clear example of a venue that discussion of such potentially harmful ideas ought to be allowed is that of a University or any other sort of educational setting where the education takes an unbiased look at the entirety of the subject the potentially harmful idea deals with rather than a propagandized one-sided approach. When clashed with the correct ideas these potentially harmful ones will easily show to be wrong in their logic.

Now, many would argue that censoring these two classifications of speech, harmful and potentially harmful, in any form would be an infringement on our first amendment as they would claim it guarantees such a right without censorship. However, the Supreme Court has already interpreted that amendment to have its own limitations and can be abridged when other interests are at stake. If slander and libel is not protected do to its lack of veracity, then the directly harmful speech ought not for its lack of veracity and its immediate harm to others. Potentially harmful speech can still be allowed satisfying a portion of free speech to still exist amongst speech of its kind. Limiting free speech has such a negative connotation that advocates for free speech will use the phrase as a pejorative tag-line without expanding on addressing the problems that arise with fully free speech. Therefore, as long as the harms of full free speech outweigh the harms of partial censorship, infringing upon the right will be necessary.

Chapter Four - Marijuana

There are many stock arguments for the prohibition of narcotics. Many of these arguments are valid but many also have flaws to them. The main debate in drugs today is the topic concerning legalization of marijuana. From a legal standpoint, Justice Spiegel gives the best exposition of the main arguments against the legalization of Marijuana and why it is in the states best interest to prohibit its use in his opinion in Commonwealth v. Joseph D. Leis.

When looking at a law which inhibits personal freedoms we must look to see if the harms of allowing the freedom outweigh having the freedom itself. Justice Spiegel gives us three harms in hopes that at least one of them will stick and therefore tip the weight of the scale in favor of outlawing marijuana. Therefore this question must be answered in three ways as it must touch each of Spiegel's harms.

The first harm is that of triggering "psychotic breaks" however this cannot in itself be considered a harm to city. If all "psychotic breaks" were harmful to society than hypnosis would not be viable. However, hypnosis is therefore "psychotic breaks" themselves are not harmful to society. The only argument, weak as it may be, that can be drawn from having this as a harm is to say it is bad for the individual, but that is not even a valid argument to make for writing a law as the law is written to protect society from actions of the individual not to protect the individual from themselves. This would be the same as the society writing a law against breaking into one's own house or one's own car. Sure there may be laws against insurance fraud but that is only when the action affects the society not when the individual is acting against themselves. It has not been proven by Justice Spiegel that "psychotic breaks" affect society therefore we cannot accept this as a harm.

The second harm is that marijuana can be a gateway drug as it will lead to people taking LSD and heroine. This is a poorly drawn conclusion as any data collected to prove this point can easily be nullified with the simple argument that the type of people who use marijuana illegally have the same personality that attracts them to other drugs. This is because the sample collected is of people who tried a new drug illegally therefore they wouldn't have as much trouble trying another drug illegally since the first drug was seemingly harmless. With this reasoning, the only reason marijuana is a gateway drug is because it is illegal and keeping such a seemingly harmless drug illegal devalues the illegality of more harmful drugs increasing the likelihood of their use. Therefore the gateway argument actually works against Justice Spiegel's point showing how it is a harm to keep marijuana illegal.

The last harm is that marijuana causes motor-vehicle accidents. This is the most valid of the harms set forth by Justic Spiegel as it truly does harm society. However, he is using an axe where a scalpel ought to be used. It could be argued that since using cellular phones on airplanes interferes with the TCAS system and can cause midair collisions that all cell phones ought to be banned. However, it is not the cell phone itself that is the evil rather it is its combination with the airplane. There is an FAA regulation against using a cell phone on an airplane and so there ought to only be a law against using marijuana while in a vehicle. The problem would be more directly addressed and the liberty would be upheld. Therefore, all of Justice Spiegel's harms have been rationally addressed.

Chapter Five - Abortion

Arguably the most controversial Supreme Court decision of the 20th Century is that in the case of Roe v. Wade. The uproar it brought about from a conservative right was only eclipsed by the turbulence from the decade before. In this case we see two different groups taking the stage to argue and give a climactic clash of ideologies. On one side you have those who argue pro-life and see this is as no-contest. On the other side you have those who see the complexities of the issue and will argue that they appreciate life, but believe a woman ought to have the right to control what happens to her body.

The argument of choice derives from the ideology of individualism and autonomy from the state. As with all ideas that seek to moderate themselves to prevent to radical and to difficult a platform to defend, individualists will argue that a person ought to be completely autonomous in their decision making so long as it does not infringe upon the rights/autonomy of another. This is limit which even the school of thought places upon the freedom as total autonomy would lead to a more radical dystopian society of people robbing, murdering and raping others for their own pleasure and justifying it through autonomy.

So it is established, then, that the right of choice is to be curtailed when it infringes on other rights. However, just because some individuals ought to have autonomy and freedom of choice does not mean that all individuals ought to have equal autonomy. Prisoners, for example, lose this right when they show that they cannot be trusted to not infringe upon the rights of others when they are given autonomy. Also, children cannot have the full rights of choice since they are not yet mature enough to make correct decisions without the guidance of their parents or guardians.

Now, at no point does a child ever have the possibility of losing their right to life and at no point is it acceptable to rob our molest a child for one's own self-interests even though the child has no autonomy. So therefore, it is clear to see that even though a person cannot make decisions on their as a child they still ought to have their basic rights of freedom from oppression protected. To go further, if a couple decided that they could no longer support a three child family (financially, mentally or by any other means) the couple would not be able to deem the child a burden and execute him/her.

So we can see common ground now on the controversy. The issue at hand here is whether a person's rights cease to exist when it lives inside another human being and whether that growth dependent on the mother is in fact a person. It is easy to see with the reasoning laid out in the previous paragraphs that if there is the life of a human being, no freedom of choice ought to allow the mother or anyone the right to abort it as it would be infringing upon the rights of another, even if that other cannot practice autonomy. Therefore, the argument then hinges on when life begins.

Some would argue that life begins when the fetus gains features similar to an adult human being such as finger nails and a heartbeat. However, this seems to be an arbitrary starting point as they are merely physical features which we can relate to. Others would argue that the birth of a child marks the beginning of life. However, this also seems incorrect as there is little physical difference in the child when they are in the womb late in the pregnancy and when they are just newly born. Also, if a person is born prematurely, then they are considered a person meaning that a fetus in the womb at the same stage as the prematurely born person must also be considered a person.

All the theories for a starting point to life during after the point of conception seem to have a reasoning based upon physical functionality. However, if an adult person does not have finger nails, they are still considered a person just as if a human being cannot make rational decisions they are considered a person. A human does not lose their humanity while they are sleeping because they do not perform typical human functions like writing sonnets, playing music or having a conversation. Therefore, we cannot attach typical human functions to the requirements of being a human being alone. Instead we must look at another standard.

The best standard for looking at someone's humanity is to see whether or not the person has the potential to write a sonnet, play music or have a conversation. Because a sleeping human being has the potential to wake up and do any one of these from an abbreviated list of typical human actions then it is obviously human. Even if the person has just fallen asleep they still have human life as it is not loss due to the time between the potential actions and the actions themselves.

Therefore we must look to see when the fetus begins to have the potential for human actions and we find where life begins and where it becomes a human being. Because a sperm and egg by themselves have no possibility of ever performing human actions they will never be considered human beings and as such ought never be given rights. However, the moment the two meet and create the chain reaction that cannot be stopped without the interference of something contrary to nature, the mixture becomes a human life as it then has the imminent potential to perform human actions. It does not matter how long it will take for the person to perform their actions, the fact is that they will someday do so without interference.

Therefore, it is reasonable to conclude that the fetus of a woman does have human life and therefore is an person which, although unautonomous, ought not have their rights infringed upon for the sake of someone else's self-interests. It has also been previously established that although a postnatal child may be a burden to its parents, the parents do not have the freedom to end the child's life due to their own right to personal choice. Even if the child is conceived through rape or incest, it is not reasonable to justify killing it. Similarly it is not reasonable then to justify killing a prenatal child since it has been established that it has the same right to life as any other human.

Now, it is clear to see that a real problem is presented with the cases of rape and incest. However, as evil as these acts are, they are not remedied by the act of infringing upon the right to life. Using abortion to solve this problem is not the answer. However, this is not enough as their is a still a problem to be solved. Therefore a possible solution to the abortion dilemma is for the medical community to make ready and affordable a device which will mimic the womb of a mother for a fetus allowing the fetus to live and the mother to be rid of a child she may not want. This would be similar to giving a live child up for adoption. This would not make everybody fully happy, but perhaps it could be the settling compromise to a heated debate.

Chapter Six - Criminals

Most of us have committed a crime at least once in our lifetimes. Whether that crime be tapping the brakes at stop sign, exceeding the speed limit or shoplifting a toothbrush which has been approved by the American Dental Association. It is easy to see that we as human beings naturally have trouble following all the rules. However, although we may have trouble it is usually with ones that are miniscule and we'd still like to think that everyone could play by the rules and abide by the laws our government has set up.

Now, since some people have trouble with the laws that are more serious than vehicular violations, but we would still like them to obey all laws, it is in our best interest to find ways to get them to live by society's standards. Some would say they are nothing to worry about. Simply keep catching them and locking them up. The problem with this notion is that over ninety percent of all inmates will eventually be released someday. When they do reenter society it is best that we aim to prevent them from becoming repeat offenders needlessly creating more victims.

One of the worst types of crime today that creates havoc amongst our society is gang related crime. Two reasons have been sited as the causes for such activity. The first is the camaraderie that is often sought after. The second is a way out of the current that is being lived. If this holds true, then the solution to gang related activity is to provide alternative routes for the two objectives sought after and to make them appealing selling them on the points that they are safer, morally superior and will make them happier in the long run.

The first change that must be made is current practices of barring those with past convictions from employment. This the most obvious change to make. Limiting the job opportunities of those who have been convicted is a counterproductive exercise. This only makes it harder to conform these convicts to proper and lawful behavior as it shows that a life of a crime is the only option for these people who are trying to be ordinary citizens. Therefore, it is in the best interest of society to prevent discrimination on the basis of prior convictions.

Now this will be something which will be difficult to pass through in legislation as many people have the view that it is best to keep the convicted unemployed as that will limit the convicts' contact with the people who have the view. However, we must look at this rationally and not through the lens of fear. Only then can we rationally solve the issue of crime alleviating its burden on society.

Chapter Seven - Education

A common assertion is that our current education system is not working. Another is that it is not working well enough. Whatever the assertion, there is generally not the consensus that the way education in America is how it ought to be and that the status quo is fine. Therefore, we must look at the entire system with a critical eye trying to find the problems and solving the the problems we find.

Some would advocate increasing teacher's pay or spending more on education by way of increased technology. These remedies by themselves will not solve the problem. The problem lies deeper, within the method of teaching and learning. Today, the mainstream of students that are not privileged enough by luck and the discriminating "honors" classes are taught merely to recite and regurgitate facts for tests and and quizzes rather than learning to apply them in problem solving situations.

The phrase "when am I ever going to use this in life" sounds as though it is nails on a chalkboard to many teachers. However, it is imperative that the students know the importance of the subject in order to be socially and intellectually functional citizens of our nation. An English can say that the interpretations of an F. Scott Fitzgerald novel are important to having deeper discussions with those around you avoiding the superficial subjects of weather and the sort. It is important to stimulating the mind.

Everything learned through the education system ought to be a means to achieving the ends of stimulating the mind. Recitation does not do this, but ponderance and problem-solving does. Formulas ought not be handed to students in math classes. Rather the student ought to figure ought the formula for his or herself. It is through the problem solving that we sharpen the tools necessary to unlocking more knowledge in the future.

The role of the teacher ought to be that of a guider, the training-wheels on a bicycle. The teacher ought never fully give the student the answer. Even in subjects where memorization of facts seems imperative such as history, comprehending the importance and the causes for landmark events and applying them to current issues is paramount to the full education of the student. The teacher ought to ask thought provoking questions concerning the events, highlighting the problems, and the student ought to answer those questions solving such problems.

The student ought to be slowly learning to find the problems and figuring ought ways to solve them. This is how progress should be measured in a student's learning, not by forcing the student to recite trivial facts with a bubble-in multiple choice answer document. Their should instead be short answer questions that incite thought within the student, pressing a problem before him that he must solve. The grade should not be based upon the correctness of the answer alone, but also on creativity, issue recognition and clearly drawn thoughts. To prevent an unfair advantage in the area of handwriting, typing ought to be utilized.

Trivial requirements, such as page length minimums for papers and other such homework and class work, should not be used by the teacher since "trivial requirements" do not provoke thought as much as recitation and robotic action. Using such requirements only dampens the morale of the student making them less willing to work hard and learn to the fullest of their capability. This clearly ought to be avoided.

The school's responsibility is to expand the learning opportunity of the student. The responsibility is not to make money or to give the appearance of a greater opportunity but to give true greater opportunity. Diverting school funds to concentrate on several intro courses from deeper more advanced courses is irresponsible and administrators who practice such acts are obviously not competent enough to handle their duties. Spraying several superficial ideas into students is as effective as throwing seeds onto a patch of dirt. In order for the courses to have any worth, time must be taken to dig deeper for the seeds, submerging them into the dirt rather than aimlessly throwing them and hoping that something will stick. When each seed or course is treated with the utmost care it will grow to produce bountiful fruit. This is how our education system must be viewed.

Chapter Eight - The Supreme Court

"Judicial Activism" is a phrase which is thrown around as a political point that many claim to be against. However, as pejorative sounding of a term it may be, it is prudent to look more closely at what the action entails. Judicial activism is anytime a partial judge or justice makes a ruling based upon how he/she believes the law ought to be without giving written statutes, codes, constitutions and briefs as much weight as his/her own opinion.

On face value this may seem wrong, but we must realize that such cases as Brown v. Topeka Board of Education are often viewed as judicially active as the Court went against the precedent set forth by Plessy v. Ferguson without any new constitutional amendments to support such a departure from the previous decision. The only new element was the "new science" presented in the case that showed the psychological effects of segregation. This went against the principal of Stare Decisis and created a mess in the court.

It was the court legislating from the bench that integration should be the policy of the South.

So then why would that be such a wrong thing? The legislature has its purpose, the executive has his/her purpose and the judiciary has its purpose. The courts ought only look at the arguments from both sides weigh them, and see where the truth lies in answer to the question asked of them. In many ways, the role of the entire judiciary is similar to that of the Whig Party.

The moment the judiciary is allowed to inject its beliefs by way of bias rulings, the flood gates slowly begin to open allowing unfair play. A judge or justice is to be much like an umpire in a baseball game. The umpire does not make a call of out or safe based upon which team he would prefer win. He does not make his decision on whether the crowd will riot or not in response. He does not weigh the moral character of either team in his decision. Rather the decision is based upon the standard agreed upon for him to use. In the case of Supreme Court Justices and lower court judges, the actual wording of the constitution ought to be used in constitutional disagreements and other statutes pertaining to the question at hand ought to determine the decision. This is the only way to keep fairness in the system because without such strict adherence to an agreed upon standard, the system has no integrity.

Chapter Nine - Affirmative Action

On college campuses across America you can always hear the complaints of seemingly privileged students not gaining the same amenities and leeway that seemingly disadvantaged students are given. This complaint has extended to beyond on college campuses and has arisen as question to many who have not gotten a certain position or promotion they wanted when another who was of a different race did. Therefore, it is prudent that we take a closer look at Affirmative Action since it has been brought into question.

The reasoning for Affirmative Action was to level the playing field for a disadvantaged minority in America. President Johnson of Texas once likened African-Americans' position in America to a shackled runner in a race. When placed into terms like this, Affirmative Action seems justified, but only to make fair what is not. Once everyone has a fair opportunity, though, it is best to make the decision of scholarships, promotions and job positions based upon merit and not factors that the actor cannot control such as race or sex.

Because of Affirmative Action's existence in today's post-civil rights world, racism still has the possibility of reemerging. When one group is put at a disadvantage to another, the disadvantaged group inherently will harbor jealousy towards the group reaping the benefits whether that beneficiary wants things that way or not. We can see this today whenever a minority excels in his or her field. The successes are automatically blamed on the individuals disadvantage and not their merits.

Rush Limbaugh's remarks about Donovan McNabb were that he only received attention due to the color of his skin. Regardless of whether this was true, the presence of an Affirmative Action sentiment in our society has a created a cloud over any minority's successes. The reason why the cloud is placed over the success regardless of whether the minority received unfair help is because all too often, others have seen the fruits of their labor overlooked for due to the color of their skin. This is where the modern racism is born.

When a student at a high school applies to a local top college but does not get in even though he is the high school's valedictorian and then finds out that a black girl with lower grades got into the college, all that can be said to the valedictorian is that he tried his hardest and their was nothing he could've changed. The valedictorian will then have resentment towards the disadvantaged group of black females for a good while. He will blame any success the group as a whole has on the same unfair advantages he saw in high school. This resentment may even evolve into hatred.

Beyond the obvious notion that Affirmative Action mentality is unfair as it does not reward work and motivation as much as uncontrollable factors, the ideology only breeds more racism -- a counterproductive action, not affirmative.

Now it is callous to turn a blind eye to the disadvantaged and act as though giving them nothing is the correct form of action. Everyone ought to have the same opportunity to produce the same results, but they ought not have the same results. That is to say, we as a society and as a nation ought to ensure that the disadvantaged have the same tools as all others to build their own future. Now, some may define "tools" as education and may point to the valedictorian anecdote as justified since the black female needed was only acquire the same tools. This would not be justified since the two students went to the same high school and so had the same tools. Success ought to derive from work not birth.

Chapter Ten - Using a Federal Government

It seems as though many have forgotten why we are the government we are. We could be have an empirical or confederate form of government in which the national government either has complete control or the states are relatively autonomous. However, we have neither of these extremes, only a hybrid of sorts, a happy medium.

In recent politics, though, the national central government has gained more and more of a hold on the power of policy making in our country. I do not say this to scare anyone with "government takeovers." I simply say it so that we can get our nation back on track. Afterall, a federal structure of government has many perks to it. These benefits are what persuaded our government's framers to choose this structure.

When coming a to a pool that has an unknown temperature, it is best to dip a toe or some other limb into the water to test the unknown. This way if the water is too hot or cold only one limb feels the effects for a short time. Whereas, if you were to jump in the pool, the entire body would feel the extreme heat or cold to a degree unbearable.

This is much like how our federal government is to be. If we are to come with a new policy with effects unknown, it is best to let the states try out and to dip them into the new ideas one at a time rather than making the entire nation jump into the unknown. Such an approach can and ought to be taken today with certain controversial issues as health care reform. There ought not be a nationwide public option before states test out the viability and effects of such a public option. This takes out the fear of the unknown that prevents much progress. The successes of the states that the national government observes can then be implemented into a nationwide policy.

Therefore, at this point in American government, it is best to push for more states' rights. That is not to say states' autonomy as the national government should still supersede the states; it is only to say that we need the states to legislate their own new ideas and for the government to only implement the ones that have shown to work and not new ones themselves.

States also ought not be coerced into implementing policies that they disagree with. Such is the case with Louisiana's wish to keep the drinking age down at 18 against the wishes of the national government. Due to this the national government withheld funding from the state. If Louisiana had not had the burden of paying for its bills without subsidies from the national government, it might not have had a compelling enough reason to raise the drinking age. Because the state will never know it will always resent the impure reasoning and coercion by the national government. The ends of raising the drinking age did not justify the means of infringing upon states' rights. If the precedent is set, than perhaps the national government will be able to force a state to implement a policy which it sees as clearly fallacious.

Similar to the Louisiana anecdote, some states are attempting to legalize marijuana. However, if they do accomplish this legalization, the national government will continue to force the marijuana ban onto the states, infringing upon their rights. Instead of allowing the states to see the effects of such a policy within the containment of the state, the government does not even allow the test to take place. Therefore, we can never truly know whether a ban on marijuana is a good policy or not in actuality.

The national government needs to be a little less hands on with the states. The state governments ought to lead innovation. Only this way can we best use our federal government.

Chapter Eleven - Taxes

The great Albert Einstein once said that among the many complexities of the world, the one thing he does not understand is taxes. Many resent and even hate taxation. This hatred has been the cause of such things as the American Revolution, the Tea Party movement and such promises as "No new taxes!" So if nobody enjoys paying taxes, why do we continue doing it without looking for an alternative?

A financial advisor will tell a family to save up in the event that the economy takes a turn for the worse and the provider(s) for the family loses his/her job. The financial advisor may also tell a family to invest in the long term with mutual funds and stocks and bonds so that the provider(s) may one day retire and not have to rely on his/her job as a sole source of income.

Similarly, the United States of America ought not rely solely on taxation as its main source of income. Instead we as a nation should be saving up tax money to do a so-called "retirement" later on in our nation's existence. First and foremost, our government, nor any government, should operate in the red. The government ought not outspend what it can generate as income. This is common sense for any family and it ought to be a centerpiece for our government.

Now, our government ought to invest a good portion of the money that is collected in taxation into other assets. We ought to buy bonds for other nations. The government can make a fortune off of high interest bonds in countries such as Greece, Ireland and Portugal. The interest that our nation generates can be used to fund programs we need while trimming down our taxes. This may sound too good to be true, and so it does have its negative drawbacks worth noting.

People do not like to pay for anything they perceive as free. Therefore, it isn't best to completely eliminate taxes where they currently exist because those tax dollars may still be needed down the road. However, this drawback can easily be addressed by simply reducing taxes to in all fields and perhaps even rotating the type of tax that takes on a heavy increase.

With lower taxes, tax cut incentives may become less enticing. This will mean that certain things as creating jobs and lowering greenhouse gas emissions may be harder to promote in corporations. Perhaps, if the government decides to replace these tax incentives with either subsidies or fines, the same effect would still be felt motivating these companies to do what our government wished.

Another drawback is that profiting off of our lending money to foreign countries may strain our relations with these debtor nations. This may be true and our government, if it undertakes this alternative to taxes, should not invest in countries known to have radical nationalists that will commit terrorist acts to liberate their country from debt.

However, if our government really can pull of this alternative form of income, we as citizens of the United States of America can finally have what we have always wanted, a world with minimal taxation.